P9-EKY-975

The Great Lakes

Erinn Banting

Weigl

CALGARY
www.weigl.ca

Published by Weigl Educational Publishers Limited
6325 – 10 Street SE
Calgary, Alberta, Canada
T2H 2Z9

Web site: www.weigl.ca

Library and Archives Canada Cataloguing in Publication

Banting, Erinn, 1976-
        The Great Lakes / Erinn Banting.
(Canadian geographic regions)
Includes index.
ISBN 1-55388-143-5 (bound).--ISBN 1-55388-150-8 (pbk.)
        1. Ontario--Geography--Textbooks. 2. Great Lakes
Region--Geography--Textbooks. I. Title. II. Series.
FC3061.2.B35 2005   917.13   C2005-904564-7

Printed in the United States of America
1 2 3 4 5 6 7 8 9 0   09 08 07 06 05

CREDITS: Every reasonable effort has been made to trace ownership and to obtain permission to
reprint copyright material. The publishers would be pleased to have any errors or omissions brought
to their attention so that they may be corrected in subsequent printings.

COVER: Lake Erie and Lake Ontario are connected by the Niagara River, which contains Niagara Falls.

Cover: Photodisc Collection/Photodisc Blue/Getty Images (front); Jan Kopec/Stone/Getty Images
(back); **Getty Images:** pages 3 (Richard Olsenius/National Geographic), 4L (Steve Bly/The Image
Bank), 4ML (Paul Nicklen/National Geographic), 4MR (Philip & Karen Smith/Stone), 4R (Francesca
York/Dorling Kindersley), 5L (Raymond K. Gehman/National Geographic), 5M (John Dunn/National
Geographic), 5R (Ed Simpson/Stone), 6 (Jan Kopec/Stone), 7 (Toyohiro Yamada/Taxi), 11 (Lawrence
M. Sawyer/Photodisc Green), 13L (Ryan Beyer/Stone), 13R (David Fleetham/Taxi), 14 (Hulton
Archive), 15L (Bryan Mullennix/Iconica), 15R (L. Lefkowitz/Taxi), 16 (Hulton Archive), 17 (Hulton
Archive), 20 (Melissa Farlow/National Geographic), 21 (StockTrek/Photodisc Green), 22 (Francesca
York/Dorling Kindersley), 23 (Fred Hirschmann/Science Faction), 24 (Raymond Gehman/National
Geographic), 25 (Medford Taylor/National Geographic), 28 (Wallace Kirkland/Time Life Pictures), 29L
(Frank Cezus/Photographer's Choice), 29R (Oliviero Olivieri/Robert Harding World Imagery), 30
(Lori Adamski Peek/Stone), 31 (Geoffrey Clifford/The Image Bank), 32 (Edu Lyra/SambaPhoto), 33
(Cosmo Condina/Stone), 34 (Altrendo), 35 (Altrendo), 36 (Jim Stamates/Stone), 37 (Jeremy
Woodhouse/Photodisc Green), 38 (Bill Pugliano/Stringer), 39 (Jerry Driendl/Taxi), 40 (Francesca
Yorke/Dorling Kindersley), 41 (StockTrek/Photodisc Green), 42 (Nancy Simmerman/Stone), 43TL
(Getty Images/Taxi), 43TR (Nicholas Veasey/Photographer's Choice), 43ML (Tom Schierlitz/The Image
Bank), 43MR (Bill Greenblatt/Liaison), 43BL (Maria Stenzel/National Geographic), 43BR (Bryce Flynn
Photography Inc/Taxi), 44L (Stockdisc/Stockdisc Classic), 44M (Ryan McVay/Photodisc Green), 44R
(C Squared Studios/Photodisc Green), 45L (Tom Schierlitz/The Image Bank), 45R
(Stockdisc/Stockdisc Classic); **Photos.com:** pages 18, 19.

Substantive Editor
Arlene Worsley

Copy Editor
Heather Kissock

Designer
Terry Paulhus

Layout
Kathryn Livingstone
Gregg Muller

Photo Researchers
Annalise Bekkering
Jennifer Hurtig

We acknowledge the financial
support of the Government
of Canada through the Book
Publishing Industry Development
Program (BPIDP) for our
publishing activities.

CONTENTS

The Regions of Canada

Canada is the second largest country on Earth. It occupies an enormous area of land on the North American continent. Studying geography helps draw attention to the seven diverse Canadian regions, including their land, climate, vegetation, and wildlife. Learning about geography also helps in understanding the people in each region, their history, and their culture. The word "geography" comes from Greek and means "earth description."

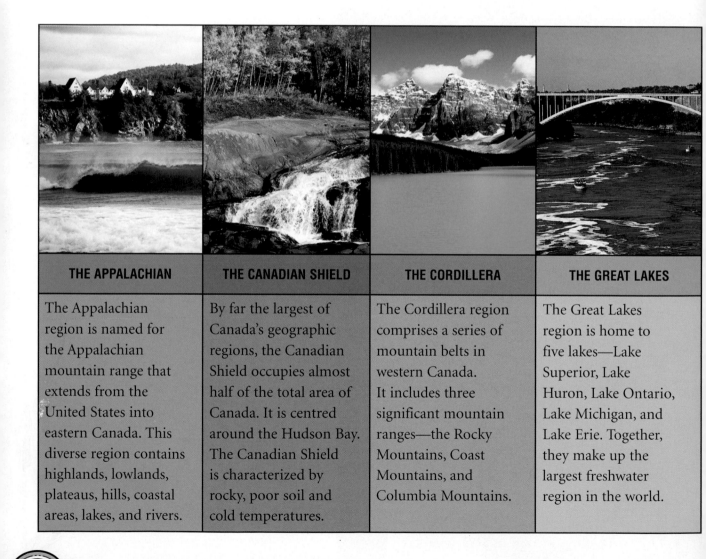

THE APPALACHIAN	THE CANADIAN SHIELD	THE CORDILLERA	THE GREAT LAKES
The Appalachian region is named for the Appalachian mountain range that extends from the United States into eastern Canada. This diverse region contains highlands, lowlands, plateaus, hills, coastal areas, lakes, and rivers.	By far the largest of Canada's geographic regions, the Canadian Shield occupies almost half of the total area of Canada. It is centred around the Hudson Bay. The Canadian Shield is characterized by rocky, poor soil and cold temperatures.	The Cordillera region comprises a series of mountain belts in western Canada. It includes three significant mountain ranges—the Rocky Mountains, Coast Mountains, and Columbia Mountains.	The Great Lakes region is home to five lakes—Lake Superior, Lake Huron, Lake Ontario, Lake Michigan, and Lake Erie. Together, they make up the largest freshwater region in the world.

Canada is home to a variety of landforms. The country hosts sweeping Arctic **tundra**, fertile lowlands, rolling plains, majestic mountains, and vast forests. Each region has a wide range of plants, animals, natural resources, industries, and people.

THE INTERIOR PLAINS	THE NORTH	THE ST. LAWRENCE LOWLANDS
The rolling, low-lying landscape of the Interior Plains is the primary centre for agriculture in Canada. The Interior Plains region lies between the Cordillera and the Canadian Shield.	Much of the North region is composed of thousands of islands north of the Canadian mainland. Distinctive landforms in the region include Arctic lowlands and polar deserts. Glacier mountains are also a recognizable feature in the North.	The St. Lawrence Lowlands region is located on fertile soil surrounding the St. Lawrence River. The region contains a waterway system linking Canada and the United States to the Atlantic Ocean.

The Mighty Great Lakes

The Great Lakes region includes the Great Lakes and the land around them. Situated along the southern part of Ontario, the Great Lakes make up part of the Canada–United States border. The smallest Great Lake is Lake Ontario. The largest Great Lake is Lake Superior.

Connecting the Lakes

The lakes are connected by a series of channels and rivers, some of which are man made. The Erie Canal, for example, was built to create a faster trade and shipping route between Buffalo and Albany, New York, and the St. Lawrence River.

> " The Great Lakes waterway has been crucial to the people, industry, and history of Canada and the United States. "

Many of the connecting waterways are natural, including the St. Mary's River. This 97-kilometre river connects Lake Superior with Lake Huron. Lake Huron is joined to Lake Michigan by the Straits of Mackinac. Lake Huron and Lake Erie are connected by a 144-kilometre channel that includes the St. Clair River, the Detroit

Founded in 1793 on the shore of Lake Ontario, Toronto and its surrounding areas have become the most productive region in Canada due partly to their easily accessible waterways.

River, and St. Clair Lake. The Niagara River connects Lake Erie and Lake Ontario. Before the waterway reaches the ocean, it rushes over world-famous Niagara Falls. Lake Ontario is the most easterly lake in the Great Lakes system. It flows to the Atlantic Ocean by way of the St. Lawrence River.

The Great Lakes waterway has been crucial to the people, industry, and history of Canada and the United States. The region has long been home to much of Canada's population. Hundreds of First Nations groups have called the region home for thousands of years. Their traditions of hunting, art, and storytelling have been influenced by the lakes and the lands around them.

Visitors to Niagara Falls can take boat tours of the area.

Connecting Canada

The Great Lakes region is one of the most populated regions in both Canada and the United States because of the large cities on its shores. The area is also a centre for agriculture. Crops such as corn, potatoes, and oats are grown in the region and are sold throughout North America and other parts of the world.

Some of Canada's largest cities, such as Toronto, Mississauga, and Brampton, are located in the Great Lakes region. These cities were built here because of the region's rich natural resources, including lumber, fish, and minerals, such as coal, iron ore, and nickel.

QUICK FACTS

- It is estimated that the Great Lakes hold more than 25 quadrillion litres of water.

- The Welland Canal, located between Lake Ontario and Lake Erie, has many locks. Locks are enclosed sections in docks and canals that are used to raise and lower ships moving between two lakes that are different heights.

- Lake Superior is the deepest and coldest of all the Great Lakes. Lake Erie is the most shallow.

Map of Canadian Geographic Regions

This map of Canada shows the seven geographic regions that make up the country. The regions are divided by their topography, from towering mountains to river valleys, and from Arctic tundra to rolling prairies. Canadian geographic regions are some of the most diverse anywhere in the world.

Studying a map of Canada's geographic regions helps develop an understanding of them, and about the nation as a whole.

YUKON TERRITORY

Gulf of Alaska

Whitehorse

PACIFIC OCEAN

BRITISH COLUMBIA

Kamloops

Victoria   Vancouver

N

W   E

S

0   500 Kilometres

LEGEND

The Appalachian

The Canadian Shield

The Cordillera

The Great Lakes

The Interior Plains

The North

The St. Lawrence Lowlands

Latitude and Longitude

Longitude measures the distance from a spot on the map to an imaginary line called the prime meridian that runs around the globe from the North Pole to the South Pole.

Latitude measures the distance from a spot on the map to an imaginary line called the equator that runs around the middle of the globe.

The Map Scale

A map scale is a type of formula. The scale helps determine how to calculate distances between places on a map.

```
0          500 Kilometres
```

The Compass Rose

North is indicated on the map by the compass rose. As well, the cardinal directions—north, south, east, and west—and the intermediate directions—northeast, southeast, northwest, southwest—are shown.

Regions of the World

Scientists who study geography look at different regions around the world that have similar characteristics, or environments. Scientists study environments to see how temperatures, animals, and plant life interact with one another. Similar regions exist in countries with very different **ecosystems** and climates.

The Story of Pangaea

The reason Earth has similar regions in different countries is that the world was once made up of one continent, or landmass. In 1912, Alfred Wegener, a German geologist and meteorologist, called this supercontinent Pangaea. He proposed the theory that Pangaea covered nearly half of Earth's surface and was surrounded by an ocean called Panthalassa. Between 245 and 208 million years ago,

> "Earth has similar regions in different countries because the world was once made up of one continent, or landmass."

PERMIAN
225 million years ago

TRIASSIC
200 million years ago

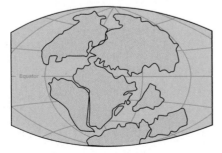

JURASSIC
135 million years ago

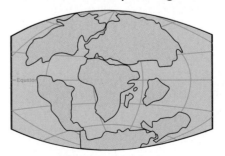

CRETACEOUS
65 million years ago

Lake Superior is the largest of the Great Lakes. It is also the largest body of fresh water in the world.

Pangaea began to separate. The pieces of the larger landmass moved apart until they formed the seven continents—Africa, Antarctica, Asia, Australia, Europe, North America, and South America.

The Great Lakes of Africa

The theory of Pangaea contends that there are similar regions on different continents because they all used to be connected.

For example in Africa, a southern continent, there is a Great Lakes region similar to the one in North America, a northern continent. The region is home to fifteen lakes in total, eight of which are considered Great Lakes because they are so large and deep. The region is also home to Lake Victoria, the second-largest freshwater lake in the world.

There are other similarities that suggest this area of Africa was once connected in Pangaea. Both the African Great Lakes region and the North-American Great Lakes have very rich soil. As a result, both areas are agricultural centres.

QUICK FACTS

- Pangaea comes from a Greek word that means "all Earth."

- The Great Lakes region of North America stretches across 151,000 square kilometres of southern Canada and northern United States.

Glaciers Shape the Land

The Great Lakes region is only 4,000 years old. This may sound old, but compared to some of the natural regions and landmarks in the world, it is very young. However, the region took millions of years to form.

> **"** The glaciers move slowly across the land. They crush and erode mountains, leaving behind soil and rocks they carried in their path. **"**

Nearly 1 billion years ago, the site of the Great Lakes was very different than it is today. Powerful volcanoes spewed molten lava over the landscape. Over time, the lava cooled and formed tall mountains. The volcanoes continued to erupt occasionally until about 5 million years ago, when the fiery land turned to a frozen landscape. This time was called the **ice age**. Earth has experienced many ice ages. During an ice age, large sections of land become covered with giant masses of ice called glaciers.

Great Lakes Formation

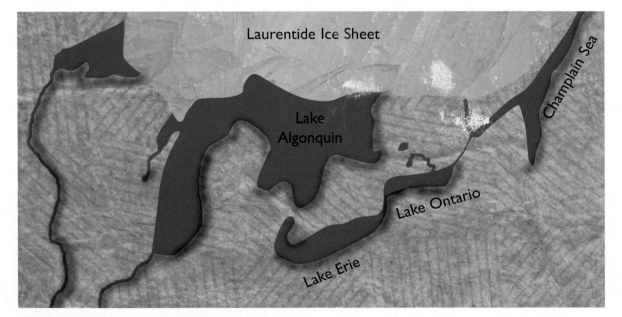

At the end of the last Ice Age, much of North America was covered by the Laurentide Ice Sheet. When the Ice Age ended, the ice sheet retreated, starting the formation of the Great Lakes.

Glaciers move slowly across the land. They crush and erode mountains, leaving behind soil and rocks they carry in their path. In the last 1.6 million years, glaciers formed and melted many times in North America. They shaped the valleys, rivers, lakes, and landscape across the Great Lakes region and the rest of Canada. When the last ice age ended, the glaciers melted and filled the area that is now the Great Lakes.

The Great Lakes partially freeze during cold winters, but only on the surface.

WHAT WAS LIFE LIKE IN THE PALEOZOIC ERA?

Imagine visiting one of the Great Lakes to snorkel in a warm sea or visit a tropical coral reef. This would have been possible during the Paleozoic era, which began more than 500 million years ago. During this era, North America experienced many dramatic changes. At this time, much of central North America was flooded by saltwater seas. Today, the Great Lakes are filled with fresh water. Freshwater fish, such as salmon, trout, and pike, live there. Millions of years ago, however, the Great Lakes region was home to several saltwater creatures. There were brightly coloured corals called "sea lilies" with long, flowing branches. Brachiopods, nicknamed "lampshades" because of their clam-like shape, also lived there.

The First Inhabitants

The indigenous peoples of Canada were the first people to live on this land. According to the traditional stories of many indigenous peoples, they have lived in North America for as long as anyone can remember. Scientists have found evidence of human activity in the Great Lakes region that dates back thousands of years.

More than 120 First Nations groups have been known to live in the Great Lakes region at one time or another. These include the Anishinabe, the Iroquois, the Ottawa, and the Potawatomi.

The First Nations in the region traditionally lived off the land by hunting, fishing, and growing crops, such as corn, pumpkins, squash, and beans, in the region's rich soil. The Ojibwa, for instance, hunted deer and harvested wild rice. First Nations Peoples feel a strong connection to the land. This is reflected in their stories and traditions.

The way of life of the First Nations was changed dramatically with the coming of European explorers and settlers. Fur-trading became an important way of life for many First Nations.

Many of the First Nations in the Great Lakes region spoke Algonquian languages. Algonquins lived in traditional homes while pursuing an agricultural way of life.

> " More than 120 First Nations groups have been known to live in the Great Lakes region at one time or another. "

Corn, beans, and squash were the staple diet of many First Nations Peoples.

Most of the land in this region became occupied with settlements as more European settlers arrived. War and disease pushed the First Nations of the Great Lakes farther west from their native land. Those who remained faced many challenges adjusting to these drastic changes.

HOW DO FIRST NATIONS PROTECT THE GREAT LAKES TODAY?

Though pollution, environmental disasters, and overfishing have reduced the number of fish in the Great Lakes, First Nations groups work diligently to protect the natural landscape. A group called The Tribes and First Nations of the Great Lakes Basin signed a document in 2004 asking the Canadian government to include the First Nations in efforts to protect the Great Lakes from environmental damage. The cultural heritage of the First Nations makes the waters of the Great Lakes very important to them. The group calls for environmental responsibility from all the people living in the region.

Arrivals from Europe

Life in the Great Lakes region changed drastically with the arrival of explorers and traders from Europe. Between 900 and 1000 AD, Viking explorers arrived on the east coast of Canada. In the 1400s, explorers began to arrive from France. Jacques Cartier crossed the Atlantic Ocean and discovered the St. Lawrence River in 1535. He claimed the river and much of the surrounding land for France. News of the abundance of furs and the hope of finding a shorter route to Asia drew more explorers from France, Great Britain, Portugal, and Spain.

" In the 1400s, explorers began to arrive from France. "

Jacques Cartier, the first European to sail up the St. Lawrence River, travelled as far as present-day Montreal.

The French travelled south and settled along the St. Lawrence River. They built forts designed to protect the settlers and the newly established trade routes that allowed goods to be shipped back to Europe.

The British eventually gained control of the area around Lake Ontario. The War of 1812 between Great Britain and the United States set the current division of the Great Lakes and surrounding region.

The naval battles during the War of 1812 established territorial divisions on the Great Lakes that continue to this day.

HOW WERE THE GREAT LAKES MAPPED?

Early maps of the Great Lakes region were not always accurate. This was partly because early explorers were not experienced **cartographers**.

Cartographers use many special tools and skills to measure and map geographic landmarks. Astrolabes, for example, were used to measure the latitude of a region. These measurements were included on maps and helped people find the location recorded by the cartographer. Compasses were also used to show cartographers and explorers which direction they were travelling.

Early maps made by explorers such as Jacques Cartier and Sebastian Cabot were sometimes incomplete or incorrect. The maps might have been incomplete because the entire region had not been explored. They were sometimes incorrect because the explorers did not have the proper tools to measure landmarks accurately. By the early 1700s, many maps had been made of the region, but there still was not one complete and accurate map.

In the late 1600s and early 1700s, a number of explorers travelled in the Great Lakes region and mapped the land. Among these was Médard Chouart des Groseilliers, who explored the region from 1654 to 1656, and from 1659 to 1660. Then, Claude Allouez explored the region from 1665 to 1667 and again in 1669. That same year, Jean Peré and Adrien Jolliet explored the region. Each of these important explorations contributed to the complete maps that exist today.

Tales of the Great Lakes

GIANT TURTLES AND MEGIS SHELLS

The Great Lakes region and the people who call it their home have a rich tradition of storytelling. Many of the stories have been told from generation to generation. Most of the First Nations groups in the Great Lakes region tell stories about how the land was created. This story tells how some First Nations came to call North America Turtle Island.

The Story of Turtle Island

Long ago, before Earth was here, all was water. Many creatures lived in the water swimming about. Far above the clouds, there was a land where lived a powerful chief. His wife was going to have a baby. In that Sky, land was a great tree with four large roots. The roots stretched out to each of the four **sacred** directions. Many kinds of fruits and flowers grew on the tree.

One night the chief's wife dreamed that the great tree had been uprooted. The chief believed this was a dream of great power. He felt it had to come true. The tree was uprooted, leaving a large hole in the Sky.

The chief's wife leaned to look through the hole. She lost her balance and fell. She grabbed at the tree as she fell, but she only managed to hold onto a handful of seeds. The water creatures below saw her falling. They saw that she was not a water creature. They tried to think of a way to help her.

"I have heard," said one, "that there is earth far below the waters.

Perhaps we should try to get some for her to stand upon."

One by one, the animals tried to dive down far enough to grab some land. One by one, they failed. Finally, a brave little muskrat dove. Her little lungs were about to burst. Suddenly she found a bit of land. She scooped it up and swam as fast as she could to the surface. Where would she put the land?

Turtle said, "Put it on my back. I will hold up the Land and the Sky woman.

So they did. Sky woman landed safely on Turtle's back. This was the origin of Turtle Island. Sky woman was very thankful. She threw the seeds about the Land. The Land became ever so beautiful. Some people eventually came to call this land North America.

The Megis Shell

According to the Chippewa Peoples, a search for the megis shell led them to settle in the Great Lakes region. Megis shells are small shells that were often used as money before Europeans arrived in North America. Some First Nations Peoples believe the first human being was brought to life when the creator breathed life into him through a megis shell. Megis shells are still used in ceremonies to heal the sick and are also worn as jewellery.

Bears

First Nations Peoples in the Great Lakes region regard the black bear as their relative and "grandmother." Although some tribes did not hesitate to kill the bear when in need of food, they sought to appease her spirit with elaborate apologies. A bear hunt was a great event, as were all hunts, to be undertaken with much preparatory ceremony.

More Than Just Lakes

Besides its deep freshwater lakes, the Great Lakes region features many other interesting landforms. The region has many beaches, sand dunes, beach ridges, wetlands, and islands.

Beaches

Most of the shoreline in the Great Lakes region is bordered by sandy beaches. Sand is created over millions of years by **erosion**. Larger rocks, mostly granite and quartz, break down until they become tiny specks of sand. The sand is washed up to the shore from the bottom of the lake by currents or waves in the water. Wind also blows sand to the beaches. Some beaches include Lake Superior Beach, Lake Huron Beach, and El Dorado Beach Preserve in the eastern basin of Lake Ontario.

Dunes

Sand dunes are normally associated with warm, dry deserts, but they are a very important part of the Great Lakes region. Sand dunes are large ridges, or hills, made of sand. They are created by wind. Sandbanks Provincial Park, situated along the shores of Lake Ontario, has the largest freshwater sand dunes in the world. Other dunes are located at Lake Huron's Sauble Beach and Lake Erie's Long Point, Rondeau Point, and Point Pelee beaches.

Some sand dunes are formed by water eroding the shoreline of the lakes and exposing debris. Wind picks up this debris and deposits it high above the shore.

Beach Ridges

Beach ridges in the Great Lakes are rocky areas covered in smaller rocks or gravel. They are ancient shorelines once covered by the waters of the Great Lakes.

Wetlands

Wetland regions, which include marshes and bogs, are essential to the Great Lakes ecosystem. Wetlands are watery areas that are not wet enough to be considered a river or lake. They are created when rivers get dammed and water from rain or melted snow becomes trapped. The marshes and bogs in the region's wetlands are home to thousands of plants and animals. Migrating birds also stop to rest and eat there during their long journeys.

Islands

There are 35,000 islands in the Great Lakes region. Some were created when sand and rocks were pushed to the surface by water currents and waves. Others appeared when water levels in the lakes lowered. The region's largest island, Manitoulin Island, covers 2,766 square kilometres on Lake Huron.

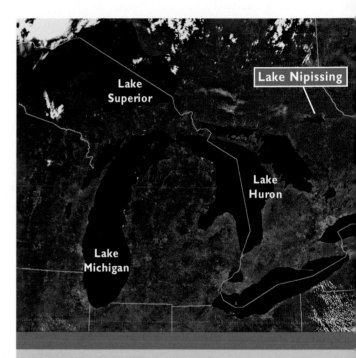

WHAT WAS LAKE NIPISSING?

Lake Michigan, Lake Huron, and Lake Superior were once part of one larger lake called Lake Nipissing. When the glaciers first melted, more of the Great Lakes region was covered in water. As the water levels lowered and the land changed because of erosion and the movements of water and wind, the lake changed and separated into the three lakes we know today.

Today, Lake Nipissing only measures 800 square kilometres. Its neighbours, Lake Michigan and Lake Huron, both measure more than 56,000 square kilometres.

Unique Landforms

The surface of the Great Lakes region also includes some very interesting land formations. Like the lakes themselves, these landforms were formed by ancient glaciers. Some of these landforms are unique to glacial regions.

Eskers

Eskers are long ridges that look like miniature mountains. They can reach heights of up to 50 metres. Eskers are created when meltwater from the glaciers moves across the land and forms small streams underneath it. Over time, the water erodes the granite below, creating the ridged areas.

66 Eskers are long ridges that look like miniature mountains. They can reach heights of up to 50 metres. 99

Niagara Falls is the world's greatest waterfall by volume, with 2,832 cubic metres of water passing over the falls every second.

Moraines

Moraines are the layers of soil, rock, and other material left behind by a glacier as it moves and melts. It picks up objects ranging in size from enormous boulders to specks of sand. The glacier then deposits these objects, creating moraines across the landscape.

Ground moraines are blankets of clay or sand 5 to 20 metres thick. End moraines are created when the edges of the glacier push rocks and other materials into piles or ridges. In parts of the Great Lakes region, there are rows of large boulders that look like a giant fence. Lateral moraines were deposited on the sides of valleys as the glacier retreated.

These stones from Lake Superior were once massive boulders, broken apart by glaciers.

Kettle Lakes

Kettles are small depressions, or basins, that form when pieces of ice break the glaciers and become trapped underground. The underground water erodes the land it settles in and eventually drains. Kettle lakes form when these large basins are filled again with water. They measure only 5 to 15 metres across.

Drumlins

Drumlins often occur in groups and look like a series of low hills rolling across the landscape. Drumlins are formed when the glacier moves over part of the land that is already covered with soil. The glacier pushes the soil into tall mounds that eventually form these hilly regions.

QUICK FACTS

> Lake Superior is so large that it could hold Lake Ontario, Lake Michigan, Lake Huron, plus four Lake Eries.

> The word "moraine" was first used in the French Alps several hundred years ago as a local name for the ridges of debris found at the edges of glaciers.

Climate in the Great Lakes

The weather in the Great Lakes region varies from day to day. The climate of the area, however, follows a predictable pattern. Climate takes into account the average temperature and the average **precipitation**. The word "climate" comes from the Greek word *klima*, which describes the angle of the sun.

The Climate of the Great Lakes

The Great Lakes region does not experience extreme weather patterns. Temperatures are neither too hot nor too cold. The region rarely experiences very wet or very dry periods, such as monsoons or droughts. The **humidity** of the region remains fairly steady year-round.

66 On average, the region sees summer temperatures range around 21° Celsius. 99

The Great Lakes have a moderating effect on the region's climate. Temperatures in the region remain reasonably stable throughout the year.

One of the most popular winter activities in the region is ice hockey, which is Canada's official winter sport.

Spring Thaw

Spring arrives in the Great Lakes region in March, when temperatures rise above 0° Celsius. Northern parts of the region still receive some snow in March. April is one of the driest months and has very low rainfall.

Summer Sun

In summer, the region experiences high temperatures. On average, summer temperatures range around 21° Celsius. Summer is also the wettest season, with average rainfall levels of 75 to 100 millimetres for June, July, and August.

Fabulous Fall

In the Great Lakes region, fall begins in the last half of September, with average daily temperatures under 16° Celsius. The first frost also comes in the fall.

Average precipitation is between 75 and 100 millimetres.

Winter Wonderland

The Great Lakes region experiences average winter temperatures between -3° and -9° Celsius. In more northerly parts of the region, record lows have reached -40° Celsius. Average snowfall varies greatly.

QUICK FACTS

- Lake Erie is the only Great Lake that regularly freezes over in winter.

- The Great Lakes act like a humidifier because they add moisture to the air. Water that is evaporated by the Sun is trapped in the air and circulated throughout the Great Lakes region.

Charting the Climate

A region's climate can indicate what it is like to live there. Temperature, snowfall, and even growing seasons are all part of climate.

Information is collected when studying a region's climate. The maps and charts on these pages help describe this information in a visual way.

Average Temperature

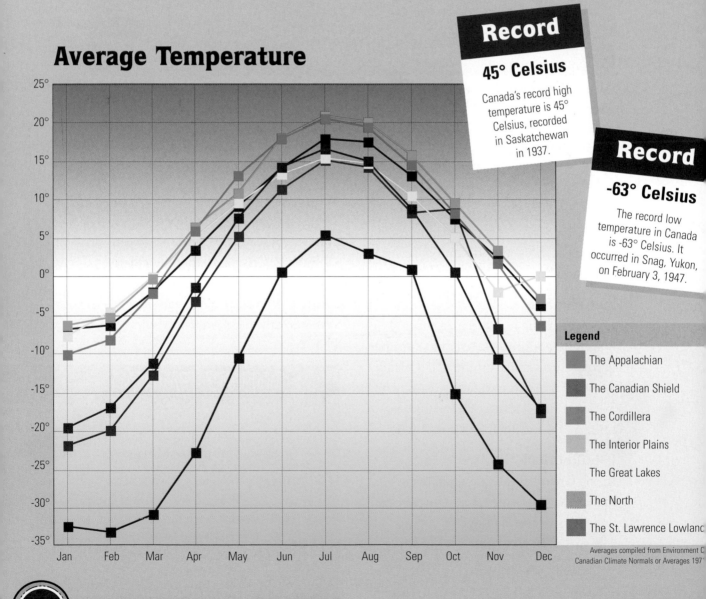

Record

45° Celsius

Canada's record high temperature is 45° Celsius, recorded in Saskatchewan in 1937.

Record

-63° Celsius

The record low temperature in Canada is -63° Celsius. It occurred in Snag, Yukon, on February 3, 1947.

Legend

- The Appalachian
- The Canadian Shield
- The Cordillera
- The Interior Plains
- The Great Lakes
- The North
- The St. Lawrence Lowland

Averages compiled from Environment C
Canadian Climate Normals or Averages 197

Average Snowfall

Legend

- over 400 cm
- 300 - 400 cm
- 200 - 300 cm
- 100 - 200 cm
- under 100 cm

Source: Canadian Oxford World Atlas, 4th Edition, 1998

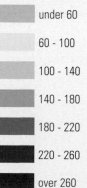

Record

118.1 cm

The record 1-day snowfall, on January 17, 1974, was 118.1 centimetres at Lakelse Lake, British Columbia.

Growing Season

Legend

Average number of days with a median temperature over 5° C

- under 60
- 60 - 100
- 100 - 140
- 140 - 180
- 180 - 220
- 220 - 260
- over 260

Source: Canadian Oxford World Atlas, 4th Edition, 1998

The Great Storm of 1913

The calm and beauty of the Great Lakes region was shattered in 1913 by a raging storm. As it blew through the region, it destroyed more than nineteen ships and took the lives of hundreds of people.

The Storm Approaches

Weather conditions in the Great Lakes region can change very quickly. Newspapers in the region on November 1913, reported cold weather with "moderate to brisk winds." By the evening of November 7, the storm had increased to a **hurricane**, with winds up to 120 kilometres per hour.

Along with high winds, the storm brought record-breaking snowfalls. Many vehicles were buried under snow. Power went out in most of Ontario, leaving residents with no electricity or heat.

> " Sailors found themselves battling 130 kilometre per hour winds and waves 10 metres high. "

Disaster on the Lakes

Radios were not common in 1913, and telegraphs did not work without electricity. News of the storm did not travel quickly. While the land was being covered in a white blanket of snow, not all ships on the lakes were alerted to the danger the storm posed. Sailors suddenly found themselves battling 130 kilometres per hour winds and waves 10 metres high. As a result, many ships sank during the 6-day storm.

The 1913 storm was unique in the region's history due to its severity.

Rain freezing on trees and transmission towers can cause them to break under their own weight.

A Deadly Toll

Wild winds, monstrous waves, and dangerous weather conditions led to the destruction of more than thirty ships on the five Great Lakes. Many of the ships were giant freighters carrying important goods.

The death toll was staggering. As many as 250 people lost their lives in the waters of the Great Lakes.

Reports on the Storm

The storm that hit the Great Lakes region in 1913 is one of the worst disasters in the history of the region. According to a report by the Lake Carriers Association in 1913, "No lake master can recall a storm of such unprecedented violence with such rapid changes in the direction of the wind and its gusts of such fearful speed!"

HOW DID THE DISASTER AFFECT PEOPLE IN THE REGION?

The greatest tragedy of the storm of 1913 was the loss of life. Hundreds of ships' crewmembers were never found. Records of the time were not as accurate as today, so the reported total of 250 is thought by some historians to be lower than the actual total.

The tragedy did not only affect the people who lost loved ones in the storm. Record levels of snow snapped power lines and forced stores to close. As a result, many businesses lost money and people had no food or water for many days. Supplies were also scarce in the region following the storm. It is estimated that nearly 1 million dollars' worth of cargo was lost in the disaster. The downed ships had been carrying coal that was used for heating people's homes, iron ore that was used for construction and manufacturing, and grain and meat, which people needed for food. Many cities and towns were left without supplies, and because of the shortage of goods, the prices of many necessities, including food, skyrocketed.

Bounty from the Land

The Great Lakes region has some of the richest deposits of natural resources in Canada. It is a key centre for agriculture, industry, manufacturing, fishing, tourism, and recreation in Canada.

Agriculture

Agriculture is very important to the **economy** of Canada. Nearly 25 percent of all crops grown in Canada are grown in the region's **fertile** soil. Common crops include corn and grains, such as barley, wheat, and oats. Farmers in the region also grow grapes and apples, which are sold throughout North America.

> "The Great Lakes region is a key centre for agriculture, industry, manufacturing, fishing, tourism, and recreation in Canada."

Mining

The glaciers that shaped the Great Lakes region also uncovered rich mineral mines. Coal, copper, zinc, gold, silver, iron ore, nickel, and lead are all mined in the region. The area also contains large deposits of natural resources used to create power or energy. Coal, once used to heat people's homes and power vehicles such as trains, is plentiful throughout the region.

Reforestation is a necessary step for conserving the region's natural environment.

Today, the mined resources are used in the manufacturing of other materials, such as steel. Natural gas and oil are also produced in the region. Uranium, which is used to create **nuclear** power, is mined on the shores of the Great Lakes.

Fishing

Fish were once the most plentiful of the Great Lakes' resources. The number of fish around the lakes has been reduced because of overfishing, pollution, and the development of cities. In Canada, about two-thirds of all fish caught in freshwater lakes are caught in Lake Erie. Trout and pike are the main species of fish caught in the lake.

Logging

Early settlers in the Great Lakes region logged the pine, spruce, oak, and maple trees in the area's dense forests. Lumber and paper made from the trees were exported to markets in Great Britain, Europe, and the United States. The region had many forests, and it was easy to transport the wood on a network of rivers and lakes. Over time, more forests were cut down to make room for growing cities. Although still important, logging is no longer the primary economic resource of the Great Lakes region that it once was.

HOW IS STEEL MADE?

Steel manufacturing is an important industry in Canada, especially in the Great Lakes region. Cities such as Hamilton, Ontario, owe their growth to the steel industry. Steel manufacturing is still very important to Hamilton and the rest of the region. Some steel is sold to factories in other countries, such as the United States. As well, much of the steel used to construct cars in Canada comes from the Great Lakes region.

Steel is made with two important substances that are mined in the Great Lakes region. These substances are coal and iron ore. To reduce shipping costs, steel foundries are built near the source of these raw materials.

To make steel, coal is heated in enormous ovens to remove impurities. The remaining substance is called "coke." The coke is used to provide energy in another large oven where iron ore is made into pure iron. The iron ore is heated until it forms a thick liquid. While it is still hot, the liquid iron is transported to yet another oven. In this oven, iron is mixed with recycled steel and other metals. The steel is then moulded into enormous slabs and further refined until it is suitable for use in manufacturing.

The Soil Underfoot

Soil is especially important to the Great Lakes region because the agricultural industry depends on it. Soil is made up of many different substances, such as rocks, minerals, decomposed plants, and other materials.

What is In Soil

Soil is broken into three layers. The deepest layer is called the parent material. This is usually made up of solid rock on which the other softer layers of soil rest. In the Great Lakes region, the parent layer is mainly rock and limestone.

> **"** The region has rich, fertile soil because of the glaciers. **"**

The layer of soil above the parent layer is called subsoil. The subsoil layer in most parts of the Great Lakes region is made of clay or sand. Topsoil, the final layer, is very fertile in the Great Lakes region.

Soil to Grow

The region has rich, fertile soil because of the glaciers. The enormous, slow-moving masses of ice not only shaped the land and carved the lakes, they also deposited the sand, rocks, and silt that make the region ideal for growing crops and forests. The minerals that are plentiful in the region were also deposited in this way and now contribute to the fertility of the soil. Finally, during the Pleistocene era, when the region was flooded by the sea, many species lived in its waters. When the sea dried up, the creatures died, and their bodies fertilized the soil.

Soil is not only essential for agriculture, it is a very important part of natural cycles that keep the region's creeks and watersheds clean.

Soil Today

Today, the Great Lakes region is still ideal for growing crops. It continues to face many challenges because of pollution, logging, and development. **Pesticides** and fertilizers are the primary cause of pollution in the region. Farmers use these chemicals to protect their crops from insects and to treat the soil so that growing conditions are optimal. However, these chemicals can get into the water supply and harm native plants and animals.

Logging has also created problems for the soil, particularly with the layers of subsoil and topsoil around Lake Michigan, Lake Erie, and Lake Ontario. The roots of trees help hold the layers of subsoil and topsoil together. When forests are cleared, there is nothing left to hold the soil together, and it quickly erodes because of water and wind. The soil is often washed away by rivers that carry it eventually into one of the Great Lakes. This makes the water level rise, as the soil settles to the bottom of the lake.

The fertile soil in the Great Lakes region is suited for growing everything from grains to fruit trees.

WHAT IS SOIL LIKE IN THE WETLANDS?

Sand and clay are commonly found in the soil of the Great Lakes region, but its large network of wetlands has created some other interesting types of soil. One type of wetland found in the region is called a bog. Bogs are formed in shallow pools. In areas where there are few rivers and streams to drain them, water collects in these pools. Plants also grow in these shallow pools and over time, they die. The plant matter **decomposes** in the pool and forms a layer of a substance called peat. Layers of peat continue to build up until the pool is filled with it. Peat was once used to heat people's homes.

Great Lakes Plant Life

In the water and on the land surrounding the Great Lakes, tens of thousands of species of plants and trees grow. From mosses to water lilies, plants are plentiful here. Even the water of the Great Lakes contains vegetation in the form of phytoplankton or algae. These tiny organisms can survive in the water without soil, by using sunlight to grow. Many insects, fish, and other organisms depend on phytoplankton for food.

66 Tall trees dominate the forests of the Great Lakes region. 99

Growing in the Wetlands

The Great Lakes region has two main types of wetlands—marshes and bogs. Marshes are located in the southern and eastern portion of the area, where the weather is warmer. Bogs form farther north and west where the weather is colder. Sedges and cattails are common in the region's wetlands. Water lilies, which have thick green leaves and large pink or white blossoms, float on the surface of the water, but are anchored, or attached, to the marsh bottom by a long stem.

Preserving the Great Lakes region's wetlands is a priority for Canadians. These ecosystems are crucial to issues such as water quality, recreation, and preserving animal habitats.

Plants on the Dunes

Sandy beaches and rolling dunes are common in the Great Lakes region. It is more difficult for plants to grow in sandy regions, but some with strong roots, such as marram grasses, plant themselves firmly in the shifting soils. The long roots of the marram grasses make it easier for other plants to grow in the sand. Other small plants, shrubs, and vines help protect the soil from erosion and attract insects that help the soil.

Plants in the Forests

Tall trees dominate the forests of the Great Lakes region. These forests are home to both coniferous and deciduous trees. Coniferous trees, such as pine and spruce trees, have needles and are green year-round. Deciduous trees, such as maple and beech trees, lose their leaves in the fall.

Maple trees are important to the Great Lakes forests. They can grow in shady forests where taller trees, such as beech trees, form a canopy and block out the sun. If a gap forms in the canopy, maple trees grow quickly to fill space. Some maple trees live to be hundreds of years old.

Many varieties of deciduous trees, such as sugar maple and beech, once dominated the forests of the region.

QUICK FACTS

- Photosynthesis is the process by which plants absorb energy from the Sun to make their own food.

- Mosquitoes often lay their larvae, or young, near the mouth of a pitcher plant. Other insects are attracted to the colour and smell of this plant. When insects approach the plant, the larvae feed on them.

- Maple trees are an important symbol in Canada. The maple leaf is pictured on the national flag. Maple sap was also important to First Nations Peoples and to early explorers, who boiled it to make maple syrup.

Animals of the Great Lakes

Animals and insects of all kinds creep, crawl, swim, climb, and fly through the many **habitats** of the Great Lakes region. The area is rich in plant life, which draws animals to live there.

Swimming in the Waves

The Great Lakes and its **tributaries** are filled with animal life. Zooplankton, a small, single-celled animal, lives in the lakes and feeds off phytoplankton. Zooplankton is food for small fish, such as smelt and sunfish, as well as other aquatic animals, such as turtles and birds. Larger fish, such as trout, pike, and sturgeon, swim in the deeper waters of the Great Lakes.

> **" The Great Lakes' watery wetlands attract millions of migrating birds each year. "**

Feathered Friends

The Great Lakes' watery wetlands attract millions of migrating birds each year. Herons, plovers, and some species of gulls are a welcome sight in spring. The V-shaped pattern of Canada geese flying high above are one of the first signs that spring has arrived to the Great Lakes region.

Amphibians and Reptiles

The lakes and wetlands in the region are also the perfect place for amphibians and reptiles. Great Lakes amphibians include frogs, toads, and salamanders. Reptiles, including snakes and lizards, also live on

Canada geese migrate long distances in the winter, travelling as far south as Mexico. During the summer, Canada geese can be found throughout Canada and the northern United States.

the shores of the Great Lakes. Snapping turtles are one of the region's most common reptilian inhabitants.

Insects

Mosquitoes lay their eggs in the wetlands and shallow parts of rivers and lakes. To many humans, mosquitoes are pests, but for dragonfiles they are an important source of food. Mantises are also common and prey on other insects, as well.

Magnificent Mammals

Mammals of all shapes and sizes roam the Great Lakes region. Red squirrels make nests in the trunks of trees where they store food for winter. On the ground, foxes and wolves look for prey. Grey wolves, also called timber wolves, once roamed throughout North America. Today, they are fewer in number and are, in fact, endangered in some areas.

One of the largest mammals in the Great Lakes region is the moose. Male moose, called bulls, can weigh as much as 725 kilograms. Black bears live in the forests of the Great Lakes region, too. They are omnivorous, which means they eat both meat and plants. The diet of these powerful bears consists mainly of berries, fish, acorns, and insects.

The moose is less social than other members of the deer family. Except during the breeding season, it is often found alone.

WHAT ARE ZEBRA MUSSELS?

Over time, humans have introduced animals to the Great Lakes that were not part of the original ecosystem. One species, the zebra mussel, has caused problems in the region. Environmentalists believe zebra mussels were introduced to the Great Lakes by a ship that had sailed to Lake Erie from the Caspian Sea in Europe. The mussels have no natural predator in the lakes, so their population quickly grew. Soon, zebra mussels were causing damage to ships, equipment, and water pipes in the lake. In addition, the mussels feed on phytoplankton, which other Great Lakes' species depend on for survival.

Region in Danger

The Great Lakes region is vital to the people, wildlife, and industry of Canada. Unfortunately, hundreds of years of manufacturing, logging, development, fishing, farming, and tourism have had a negative impact on the region.

Water Pollution

Pollution had been a problem for hundreds of years. There were few laws to stop people from polluting the waters of the Great Lakes until the 1970s. Today, Canada and the United States continue working to end pollution in the region, but it is still a problem. Some people continue to pollute the water directly by not properly disposing of waste. A more dangerous problem is runoff that carries pesticides, fertilizers, and other chemicals into the lake water systems.

> " Pollution has been a problem for hundreds of years. "

The Impact on the Environment

Water pollution greatly impacts plants and animals in the region. One example is when pesticides make their way into the water. They are absorbed by the phytoplankton that live there, and the phytoplankton become **toxic**. Then, when the zooplankton eat them, they absorb the **toxins**, as well. This continues up the **food chain** until hundreds or thousands of animals and even people are affected.

Air Pollution

Global warming is one of the greatest threats to the world's environment. It occurs when pollutants in the form

Shipping traffic on the Great Lakes can cause damaging water pollution and oil spills.

of gases become trapped in our atmosphere. Over time, the gases form a barrier that traps heat close to Earth's surface. The trapped heat warms the planet, disrupting the ecosystems. In the Great Lakes, higher temperatures have increased the rate of evaporation from the water, causing water levels to decrease. Lower water levels reduce wetland areas on the lakes' shores. Plants are destroyed along with habitats for migrating animals.

Q Should chemical pesticides and fertilizers be banned?

NO	YES
Fertilizers help farmers grow better crops. Farmers may go out of business if their crops produce poorly.	People may be eating some of the chemicals that are used on crops. These are not good for people.
Many natural pesticides do not work well at keeping away pests, such as insects and animals, that destroy farmers' crops.	Cattle and chickens may also be eating hay and other feed that have pesticides or fertilizers used on them. When people eat the meat from these animals, they may also be consuming these chemicals.
If farmers' crops produce poor yields, people in the region may suffer from a shortage of food.	Chemical fertilizers and pesticides may wash into rivers and lakes, killing or contaminating aquatic plants and animals. People may get sick from eating contaminated fish.

View from Above

There are different ways to view a region. Maps and photos, including those from satellites, help to show the region in different ways.

A map is a diagram that shows an area's surface. Maps can demonstrate many details, such as lakes, rivers, borders, towns, and even roads.

Photos can demonstrate what a region looks like close up. In a photo, specific objects, such as buildings, people, and animals, can be seen.

Satellite photos are pictures taken from space. A satellite thousands of metres in the air can show details as small as a car.

ONTARIO
Lake Nipigon
L. Superior
Sudbury
Ottawa
L. Huron
Brockville
L. Michigan
Toronto
L. Ontario
L. Erie
N W E S
0   500 Kilometres

Questions:

What information can be obtained from a photo?

How might a map be useful?

What details are indicated on a satellite photo that cannot be seen on a map?

Satellite Image of the Great Lakes

Lake Nipissing

Satellite Map Overview

Lake Superior

Georgian Bay

Lake Michigan

Lake Ontario

Toronto

Lake Huron

Lake Erie

The Great Lakes are divided across the Canada–United States. border, or the 49th parallel. To the north of this border, the Canadian provinces of Ontario and Quebec neighbour Lake Superior and Lake Huron. To the south of the border, the U.S. states of Wisconsin, Michigan, and Pennsylvania neighbour Lake Michigan, Lake Erie, Lake Ontario, and parts of Lake Huron.

What do you notice about this satellite photo compared to a regular photo? What information can you learn from it that you would not learn from a map?

Technology Tools

People have studied geology for hundreds of years. Geologists study the rocks, earth, and surfaces that make up Earth. Even before the science of geology had a name, ancient peoples studied the rocks and minerals around them. They experimented to find out what kind of rocks were used to make weapons, jewellery, and items they needed in daily life. Flint, a type of rock that is easy to shape and sharpen, was used to make spears. Minerals, such as gold and copper, were too soft to use as weapons or tools and were shaped to make beautiful jewellery.

Today, geologists use some tools that have been around for centuries, as well as more modern tools. These tools range from simple pick hammers to sophisticated computer equipment. Geologists use these tools to study the rocks and minerals they find on land. They study geology in other areas, as well. Modern technology and tools help them study geology under the sea, in volcanoes, and even on the Moon.

Careers in Geology

What information is needed to determine if geology is a good career choice?

Answer: Enrolling in introductory geology courses at university is a good way to learn about geology. Further courses will lead to 4 years of study to obtain a bachelor of science degree in geology. Working at geological jobs in the summer can help in learning about the different tasks involved in being a geologist.

Tools of the Trade

Rock hammer or pick:
These special hammers have a flat end that is used to crush larger pieces of rock, and a pointed end, which is used to pick away smaller pieces of rock.

X rays:
X rays help geologists study material in detail. Certain crystals or minerals can be examined very closely by an X ray. Geologists studying ancient fossils or artifacts also use X rays so they can examine delicate objects without damaging them.

Compass:
A compass helps geologists tell which direction they are going. Compasses are very important to geologists, who often work from maps to travel to the areas they are studying.

Seismograph:
A seismograph measures Earth's vibrations. Geologists use seismographs to study the movements of Earth's tectonic plates. Tectonic plates are huge slabs of rock that shift and move beneath Earth's surface. When two or more plates collide, there is an earthquake.

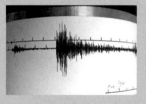

Brushes:
Some of the rocks and materials geologists study are very delicate. Once geologists have uncovered an object in the rock or soil, they use soft brushes to remove dust and debris without causing damage.

Sonar:
Sonar helps geologists map areas that cannot be reached by humans or seen by the human eye. Sonar sends out a beam of sound. Geologists determine what the sonar has hit by the type of vibration that returns. They can map these locations by listening to the sound.

What is a hydrologist?

Answer: A hydrologist is a scientist who studies the movement and distribution of Earth's waters. Hydrologists research questions about water quality, quantity, and availability. A hydrologist might study a lake or a river to learn about water level, shoreline erosion, or the flow of water from a dam.

Mapping Your Supermarket

Maps are important because they show people how to get from place to place. Geography is the study of the world's patterns, but patterns are everywhere in your daily life. The next time you go to the supermarket, try the following activity.

1. With a parent, explore the supermarket. How are things arranged? Are similar foods grouped together? Does this make it easier for people to find what they are looking for?

2. Using a grid, make a map of what is kept in each aisle. Are there aisles for special kinds of food? Is there a frozen food section? Is there a section for Asian or Mexican food?

3. When you get home from shopping, note on your map where each item was found in the store. Do you see any patterns? From which aisles of the supermarket does your family buy the most food? Are there any aisles in the supermarket you would like to visit and buy a type of food you have never tasted?

Spot the Error

To locate a certain place on Earth, mapmakers created the latitude and longitude grid. This grid is a way of dividing Earth into sections using lines that circle Earth from east to west and from north to south.

Look at the map of the Great Lakes region. Then look at the latitude and longitude coordinates for each of the locations below. Can you find the one that is incorrect?

Lake Nipissing 46°N 79°W

Ottawa 45°N 75°W

Thunder Bay 48°N 89°W

London 41°N 78°W

Sault Ste. Marie 46°N 84°W

Toronto 43°N 79°W

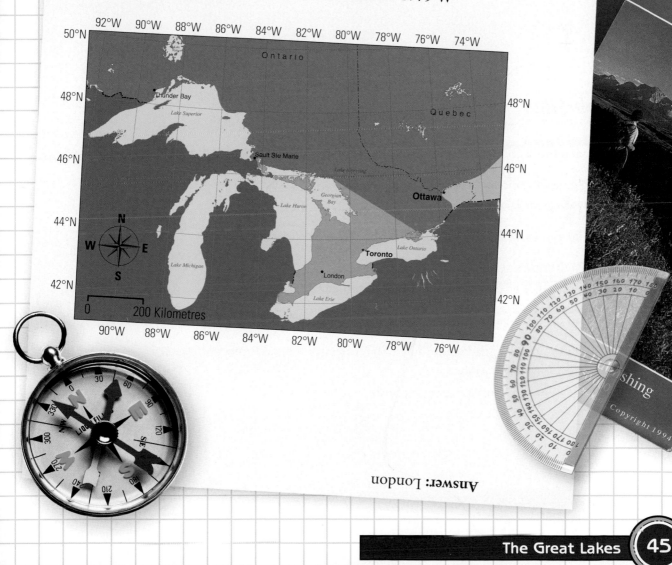

Answer: London

Further Research

Books

Find out more about the Great Lakes.

Katz, Sharon. *The Great Lakes*. Salt Lake City, UT: Benchmark Books, 1999.

St. Antoine, Sara. *The Great Lakes*. Minneapolis, MN: Milkweed Editions, 2005.

Web Sites

To learn more about the Great Lakes region, visit:

The Education and Curriculum Homesite: Great Lakes
www.great-lakes.net/teach/

To find games, activities, and quizzes about the Great Lakes, visit:

Environment Canada: Great Lakes
www.on.ec.gc.ca/greatlakeskids/glk-glinfo-e.html

To find more maps and photos of the Great Lakes region, visit:

Environment Canada and United States Environmental Protection Agency:
The Great Lakes Atlas
www.epa.gov/glnpo/atlas/index.html

Glossary

cartographers: people who make maps

decomposes: breaks down through a chemical process

economy: the structure that relates to the production, distribution, and use of goods and services

ecosystems: all of the living and nonliving things in specific areas

erosion: the process of being worn down by wind, rain, or ice over time

fertile: having the ability to, or being suitable to, grow plants

food chain: the order of organisms in relation to whether they are predators or prey

habitats: environments in which plants and animals live

humidity: the measure of how much water there is in air

hurricane: a storm that includes thunder, lightning, rain, and extremely powerful winds

ice age: period of time when the Earth is widely covered in ice

nuclear: a type of energy

pesticides: chemicals used to prevent insects and other pests from destroying crops

precipitation: the depositing of moisture in the form of rain, dew, or snow

sacred: something that is honoured because it is considered to be special

toxic: poisonous

toxins: poisonous products that originated from an animal or vegetable

tributaries: streams, rivers, or channels that connect one body of water to another

tundra: a vast, level, treeless plain

Index